KU-541-391

Can I tell you about Asthma?

A guide for friends, family and professionals

LESLEY MILLS
Illustrated by Rosy Salaman

Jessica Kingsley *Publishers*
London and Philadelphia

First published in 2013
by Jessica Kingsley Publishers
116 Pentonville Road
London N1 9JB, UK
and
400 Market Street, Suite 400
Philadelphia, PA 19106, USA

www.jkp.com

Copyright © Lesley Mills 2013
Illustrations copyright © Rosy Salaman 2013

All rights reserved. No part of this publication may be reproduced in
any material form (including photocopying or storing it in any medium
by electronic means and whether or not transiently or incidentally to
some other use of this publication) without the written permission of the
copyright owner except in accordance with the provisions of the Copyright,
Designs and Patents Act 1988 or under the terms of a licence issued by the
Copyright Licensing Agency Ltd, Saffron House, 6–10 Kirby Street, London
EC1N 8TS. Applications for the copyright owner's written permission to
reproduce any part of this publication should be addressed to the publisher.

Warning: The doing of an unauthorised act in relation to a copyright work
may result in both a civil claim for damages and criminal prosecution.

Library of Congress Cataloging in Publication Data
A CIP catalog record for this book is available from the Library of Congress

British Library Cataloguing in Publication Data
A CIP catalogue record for this book is available from the British Library

ISBN 978 1 84905 350 1
eISBN 978 0 85700 744 5

Printed and bound in Great Britain

Health Improvement
Library, Law House
Airdrie Road, Carluke
ML8 5ER
01698 377600

616.238 MIL (B)

369 0290312

Can I tell you about Asthma?

Can I tell you about...?

The 'Can I tell you about...?' series offers simple introductions to a range of limiting conditions. Friendly characters invite readers to learn about their experiences of living with a particular condition and how they would like to be helped and supported. These books serve as excellent starting points for family and classroom discussions.

This book is dedicated to all the children with Asthma and their families that I have had the pleasure of seeing in Asthma clinics throughout the country.

Acknowledgements

I would like to thank Jessica Kingsley and her team, especially Lucy, for putting their trust in me and offering me the opportunity to write this book to add to their 'Can I tell you about...?' series.

I would also like to thank Rosy Salaman for capturing the character of Alfie just perfectly in her wonderful illustrations.

Thanks also go to all the people that I have worked and studied with over the years, who have been instrumental in shaping my Asthma knowledge, enabling me to write this book.

Finally, I would like to thank my lovely family for all their patience and support.

Contents

Introduction

This book aims to help children and young people from 7 years upwards and their friends, family and professionals gain a far clearer understanding of Asthma.

- It will describe what Asthma is, explain what it feels like to have Asthma, how other people treat you and what to do in an emergency. It will also explore basic Asthma diagnosis, explaining some of the tests. It will discuss Asthma 'triggers' and Asthma medicines.

- It is a useful aid to prompt discussion both in the classroom and at home.

- The two extra sections at the back of the book offer tips for how teachers and parents can help children with Asthma.

Many teachers and parents are already very aware of Asthma and how they can help. For those teachers and parents, this book should act as a refresher and a means of support.

"I'd like to tell you what it's
like to have Asthma."

"I have had Asthma since I was very young. My mother had Asthma when she was young too, so I had double the chance of getting it.

When I was much younger I didn't understand anything about my Asthma. All I knew was that it was very frightening. Sometimes I would forget I had Asthma and run about with the other children in the park and then I would be reminded as I started to wheeze (a wheeze is a funny whistling noise you make when breathing), and I would become more and more short of breath.

I used to get so frightened I would panic and cry, which made my Asthma much worse.

It didn't always have to be running about that triggered it off. I used to hate catching a cold, as that would trigger it off too."

"I know I should try to keep calm,
because getting upset can make
it worse, but it is really difficult."

"Lots of people try to help by saying things like, 'Why don't you have a lie down?' No, I wouldn't be able to breathe at all if they made me do that. I just need to sit upright.

Sometimes it used to be so bad that I didn't have enough breath to talk. I used to be so frightened and gasping for breath and sometimes felt like I couldn't breathe at all.

The only thing that helped was my blue inhaler, but I knew I must use it with my spacer so the medicine would get into my airways to work properly. Once I had taken that, I knew it was only going to be a short time until I started to feel better.

Now that I am taking my brown inhaler regularly in the morning and in the evening, I don't have these Asthma attacks, or at least not as often. That's great news! (More to come on my inhalers on pages 23–27.)"

"I used to get teased at school
because I was frightened to
join in the games the other
children were playing, in case
I had an Asthma attack."

"The other children didn't understand and thought I was just being grumpy so they used to make fun of me. Sometimes I would get so upset that it would trigger an attack. I used to try to get out of going to school by pretending to be ill, but Mum always used to make me go.

In PE lessons the teacher used to get angry with me because she thought I wasn't trying and I was always the last one to be picked for a team.

It all made me feel so lonely and sad that I hated going to school. I just didn't know what to do and nobody seemed to understand."

"When I've been out in the street
and had an Asthma attack before,
it's been really strange to see
the way some people react."

"Many people rush past and try to pretend they haven't seen me. Then there are other people who try to help by saying they will call an ambulance immediately. I thank them, but explain that isn't necessary.

I think because a lot of people don't understand about Asthma and don't know what to do, they get very frightened.

I just need to sit somewhere calm and take my blue inhaler.

By all means sit with me and talk very calmly and reassure me. That would be great.

I think most people would like to help, but they just don't know the right thing to do."

"I usually start to feel short of breath first and then my chest starts to feel tight, as if I have a large elastic band around it squeezing me. Often, but not all of the time, I get a wheeze when I breathe out."

"Then one morning a letter dropped on the mat. Mum opened the letter. It was from a specialist Asthma nurse who was working at our doctor's surgery. She had written to Mum asking her to take me for an annual Asthma review. Mum phoned the surgery and made an appointment.

On the day of the appointment, I was a bit worried because I didn't know what they might do to me, but Mum said she felt sure it would be all right. The letter had also asked Mum to take both my inhalers to show the Asthma nurse."

"Asthma is described as a
disease of the airways (the tubes
into your lungs), which causes
breathlessness, chest tightness,
wheezing and coughing."

"When Mum took me for my annual Asthma review, I met nurse Lucy, the specialist Asthma nurse. Nurse Lucy was very patient and explained so much to me. These are some of things she told me.

When Asthma is not correctly controlled it often causes night coughing, due to inflammation (redness and swelling) in the airways.

All living creatures need oxygen (a gas from the air that helps us breathe). We can breathe in through the nose or mouth, but if we breathe in through the nose the air is warmed, moistened (made slightly wet, as very dry air might make us cough) and filtered (any nasty unwanted bits are trapped) by the tiny hairs inside our nose called cilia, which stop any bits getting into our lungs.

Once down in the lungs the oxygen is taken out of the air and used in our body and the rest of the air (the part we don't need, which is called carbon dioxide) is then breathed out.

Everyone's airways react to an inhaled (breathed in) irritant (or trigger, as it is often called), whether it be dust, smoke or anything else that irritates the airways, but when a person has Asthma their airways are more sensitive and tend to over react."

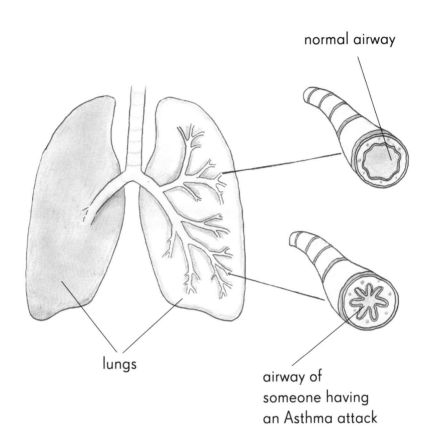

normal airway

lungs

airway of
someone having
an Asthma attack

"Triggers cause the body to
tighten the muscles around
the airways, which makes the
airways become narrower."

"The top tube in the diagram is a normal airway and the bottom tube is a narrow airway, where it is difficult for the air to get through.

The body does this to try to protect itself; but by doing this it makes it more difficult for the person to breathe and makes them feel short of breath and get that 'chest tightness' feeling and start wheezing and coughing.

Not everyone's Asthma is the same. For some people coughing may be their only symptom. Others may only need to use their blue inhaler when they have a cough or cold and some may only need it before they play sport.

If you are using your brown inhaler regularly, but still need your blue inhaler every day too, your Asthma nurse will check your inhaler technique to make sure you are taking the medicines correctly.

Asthma doesn't go away, but from the age of about 14–20 years old, it quite often goes into remission (goes away for a while)."

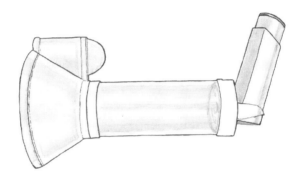

"This is what a metered dose inhaler
(MDI) and spacer look like."

"Nurse Lucy explained the difference between the blue and brown inhalers.

The blue inhaler is called a Short Acting Beta-agonist or SABA for short, but is usually known as the reliever. The blue inhaler is the one for emergency use and the one to take when you feel short of breath, are coughing, wheezing or before playing sport. The blue inhaler opens up the airways to allow more air in.

You don't have to use your blue inhaler if you don't need it, but it is very important to keep it with you at all times.

If you do need to use your blue inhaler three or more times a week regularly, or are coughing at night, then you should also have a brown inhaler.

The brown inhaler is called an Inhaled Corticosteroid (ICS). These inhalers are usually known as preventers, because they calm down all the redness, soreness and swelling in the airways and prevent you from feeling short of breath, wheezing and coughing. When you use your brown inhaler regularly, morning and evening, you don't need to use your blue inhaler as much."

"Nurse Lucy explained that it is very
difficult for young people to use
a metered dose inhaler (MDI) or
puffer on its own without a spacer."

"The medicine in the MDIs comes out at about 70 miles per hour, so if you don't start to breathe in just before you puff your inhaler, or if you puff the inhaler and then breathe in, the medicine will stick to the back of your throat and do no good at all.

If that happens with the brown inhaler it could give you a dry, sore throat or make you cough.

It is very important that after taking the brown inhaler you rinse your mouth thoroughly, or clean your teeth, as the medicine in this inhaler may make your mouth sore (although it is unusual for this to happen).

Some people leave their brown inhaler next to their toothbrush, so as soon as they have taken it, they remember to brush their teeth.

Even with a spacer if you breathe in too hard and fast the medication could still stick to the back of your throat. So if you do breathe in too hard and fast it whistles, as a warning."

"Asthma medication and spacers are now kept in a filing cabinet in the classroom."

"Nurse Lucy asked how I managed my Asthma at school.

I told her that my medicine was always locked away in the school medical room. Nurse Lucy said that wasn't right and that she would phone the school and have a talk with the head teacher.[1]

The head teacher arranged for nurse Lucy to visit one lunchtime to help the teachers understand more about Asthma. It went so well that the head teacher invited her back on several occasions to educate the pupils.

Following the education sessions, the Asthma medication is now being kept in a filing cabinet in the classroom.

Since Asthma has been explained properly to them, my classmates understand why I am sometimes worried about playing with them and encourage me to join in.

I'm so much happier at school now and my schoolwork has improved. I no longer feel 'different'. Nurse Lucy said Asthma shouldn't control our lives, we should control it."

---

[1]   The DoH recommend that all emergency medicines, such as Asthma inhalers, should be readily available to children when needed and not locked away.

"If any of you are frightened to go
and see the Asthma nurse, as I was,
I will tell you exactly what she did
and then it won't seem so scary."

"When I first went for my Asthma review I was asked some easy questions about my Asthma and me. That is called taking a history and it helped to build up a picture of my Asthma.

I was then asked to take my shoes off and stand on the scales to be weighed. Then, while my shoes were still off, I was measured to see how tall I was.

Nurse Lucy showed me a little tube, with a mouthpiece at one end and an arrow running along it. When you blow into the mouthpiece it pushes the arrow along. How far the arrow goes depends on how hard you are able to blow into it. It is called a peak flow meter. It measures how much air I could blow out of my lungs in one go. Peak flow readings are helpful to confirm Asthma. I had to stand up, take a deep breath in, seal my lips around the peak flow meter mouthpiece and blow hard and fast into it, pretending I was blowing my birthday candles out. She asked me to do that three times and then she took the best reading. I was given a peak flow meter and a peak flow diary to take home. I had to blow into it in the morning and then in the evening and record it on the peak flow diary for two weeks."

"A trigger is anything that irritates the airways, causing Asthma symptoms."

"The airways of people with Asthma appear to be more sensitive to triggers than those of people who do not have Asthma.

For young children the most common Asthma trigger is known to be coughs and colds caused by a tiny bug called a virus, and for older children the most common Asthma trigger is known to be exercise.

My main triggers are animals (mostly cats, dogs and horses), tree and grass pollens, house dust mites and when I get upset or worried.

There are many Asthma triggers. Some triggers are more common than others and everyone's Asthma triggers are different.

There is a list of Asthma triggers in the 'How parents can help' section at the end of the book.

Triggers will always be there, but we must just try to avoid them as much as we can."

"It is very important that I remember what to do in an emergency, so I have a little card written by Asthma UK that I keep in my pocket."

"There are five steps:

1. Take one or two puffs of your reliever inhaler (usually your blue inhaler) immediately.

2. Sit down and try to take slow, steady breaths.

3. If you do not start to feel better, take two puffs of your reliever inhaler (one puff at a time, shaking it in between) every two minutes. You can take up to ten puffs.

4. If you do not feel better after taking your inhaler as above, or if you are worried at any time, call an ambulance.

5. If an ambulance does not arrive within 10 minutes and you are still feeling unwell, repeat step 3."

"After an Asthma attack, always make an appointment to see your Asthma nurse or doctor, within 48 hours. Then they will usually want to see you again a week or two after that.

Be aware of the signs that may be leading up to an Asthma attack:

- If your Asthma symptoms have worsened over the past few days.

- If you are needing your blue inhaler (reliever) three or more times a week, it may mean your Asthma is not as well controlled as it should be.

- If you feel your Asthma is getting worse, or you are needing your blue inhaler more often than is usual for you, then make an urgent appointment to see your Asthma nurse or doctor.

- Don't feel you are making a fuss or being a nuisance.

- Don't wait until you have an attack – attack the problem."

Asthma facts and figures

300 million people worldwide suffer from Asthma.

In Western Europe almost 30 million people now have Asthma and this has doubled over the last decade, with estimates suggesting that Asthma increases globally by 50% every decade.

The highest rates of Asthma are found in New Zealand – 15.5%, UK – 15%, Australia – 14.7%, Canada – 14.1%, and the United States – 10.9%. Ethnic groups, such as African Americans, are even more likely to suffer from Asthma.[1]

ASTHMA PREVALENCE IN THE UK[2]

- 5.4 million people in the UK have Asthma.

- 1.1 million children (1 in 11) and 4.3 million adults (1 in 12).

- On average there are two children with Asthma in every classroom in the UK.

1   Braman, S.S. (2006) "The Global Burden of Asthma." *Chest Journal* *130*, 4S–12S.
2   Asthma UK, www.asthma.org.uk.

- 75% of hospital admissions are avoidable.
- Many asthmatics are living with symptoms unnecessarily.

ASTHMA PREVALENCE IN AMERICA[3]

- 44,000 people have an Asthma attack every day.
- 36,000 children miss school due to Asthma every day.
- 27,000 adults miss work due to Asthma every day.

ASTHMA PREVALENCE IN CANADA[4]

- Over 3 million Canadians have Asthma.
- 13% of Canadian children have Asthma.
- Asthma is the leading cause of absenteeism from school.

---

3   Asthma and Allergy Foundation of America, www.aafa.org.
4   Asthma Society of Canada, www.asthma.ca.

ASTHMA PREVALENCE IN AUSTRALIA[5]

- Over 2 million Australians have Asthma.

- 1 in 7 primary school children, 1 in 8 teenagers and 1 in 9 adults have Asthma.

- Australia has the third highest worldwide rate of current wheeze, after New Zealand and the UK. Despite this, only a small proportion of children were regularly taking their preventer medication.

ASTHMA PREVALENCE IN NEW ZEALAND[6]

- 1 in 4 children and 1 in 6 adults have Asthma, one of the highest Asthma rates in the world.

- Hospitalisation rates for Asthma have more than doubled in the past 30 years.

5   Health Insite Australia, www.healthinsite.gov.au.
6   Asthma Foundation New Zealand, www.asthmanz.co.nz.

"Wow, those facts and figures really do mean I'm certainly not the only one with Asthma!

Well I've got some facts and figures of my own...

The word 'Asthma' came from the Ancient Greeks, who used it to mean 'panting attack'.

It was described in the Chinese document *The I Ching* (*The Book of Changes*), the oldest medical work in the world (c.1000 BC), and in *The Ebers Papyrus* from Ancient Egypt (1500 BC). Asthma has plagued mankind for thousands of years, but a great number of cures used during its history have been as harmful as the condition itself. Although not perfect, our treatments today are definitely an improvement on the animal excreta (poo) from camels and crocodiles that people with Asthma were treated with in Ancient Egypt. Later, in the 17th century, treatment included horse poo and medicine made from fox's lungs.

Yuk, glad I didn't live then!"

More information about Asthma[1]

"Once I started taking the brown inhaler, it began to have an effect within about seven days. As it takes a while to 'build up' it must be taken as regularly as agreed with the Asthma nurse or doctor. This is usually twice a day – once in the morning before school and then again in the evening before bedtime.

There is no need to take the brown inhaler to school as, according to research, you get no better effect by taking it more frequently.

Many parents see the word 'corticosteroid' and worry. They often ask if it will effect the growth of their child. They confuse the tiny amount of inhaled steroid in the brown inhaler with steroid tablets that are only given for a short time when a person's Asthma is really bad, or anabolic steroids, which are more dangerous and powerful and some people take to build up their muscles. The tiny bit of steroid in these brown inhalers is just to calm down the soreness, redness and swelling in the airways and it is very important that it is taken regularly.

There are many different types of inhalers available and your nurse or doctor will talk to you about the best one for you. Usually it is the MDI that is given to younger people, for both the blue and brown inhalers. It is

---

1   Information from the National Respiratory Training Centre, Warwick.

important that you are given the same type of inhaler for both medicines, to avoid any confusion.

Many people think they are using them correctly, until their inhaler technique is checked and it is often found that they have not been receiving all of their medication.

It is recommended that young people 'always' take their reliever inhaler (MDI) with a spacer (BTS).

There are several different types of spacers, but the one most commonly used is the one that I have. It's a little clear plastic tube, which is blue at each end. It has a hole at one end to put the MDI inhaler in (after you have given it a good shake) and a mouthpiece at the other end, which you put your mouth right over. These spacers are suitable for children from 5 years old up to adults.

The correct way to use the spacer is:

1. Remove the cap.

2. Shake the inhaler and insert in the back of the spacer.

3. Place the mouthpiece in the mouth.

4. Press the canister once to release a dose of the medicine.

5. Take a deep, slow breath in (if you hear a whistling sound, you are breathing in too quickly).

6. Hold your breath for about 10 seconds and then breathe out through the mouthpiece.

7. Breathe in again, but do not press the canister.

8. Remove the mouthpiece from the mouth and breathe out.

9. Wait 10 seconds before a second dose is taken (as above).

Another technique is to do the same as above, but breathe in and out five times. This is usually a method for younger children.

There are also different spacers for younger children – an orange-ended spacer for 0–18 months and a yellow-ended one for 12 months to 5 years. Both of these have little masks which go over the mouth and nose and help the user to breathe in effectively."

How teachers can help

"I am happy at school now, but I can still remember the way I used to feel and how frightening it was.

Luckily that's all changed now, but it may still happen to someone else unless teachers understand more about Asthma and the feelings and worries of children with Asthma.

I think it would be brilliant if all teachers could have Asthma training so they understand more about it.

My mum looked up some information about school Asthma policies and told me:

- Every school should set up an Asthma policy. It is the school's responsibility and is usually taken on by the school nurse.

- All of the teachers and staff should be aware of the Asthma policy.

- If teachers need help setting up a school Asthma policy, information can be obtained from Asthma UK.

- Teachers should be aware that the NAC recommends children over 7 years keep their inhalers with them at school, so they can take them into the playground.

- My teacher should make sure my inhaler and spacer are easily accessible in the classroom or that I keep them with me – even better.

- Allow me to keep a spare inhaler at school in case the inhaler I am using runs out.

- It would also be nice to have a 'quiet area' to sit and take my inhaler and recover, maybe behind a screen in a corner of the classroom.

- It would be great if my teacher could talk to me about Asthma and ask me questions about what will help. I will then feel I can tell you about any problems or fears.

- My teacher should try to talk to my parents regularly too, so everyone knows what's going on.

- It would be really good too, if you would explain about Asthma to the other children, who may still not fully understand.

- Try to imagine just how frightening PE can seem to a child with Asthma.

There are so many things that teachers can do to help. Teachers are responsible for our care during the school day and we trust you and rely on you for your support.
   Be patient with me.
   Thank you!"

How parents can help

"Mum and Dad, it's great that you have taken the time to find out so much about Asthma. It really helps me.
It would be good if you would continue to:

- Keep updated by looking at websites such as Asthma UK (there is a list of international websites at the end of this book).

- Make sure that we attend regular Asthma reviews when we're invited.

- If I forget, remind me to take my brown inhaler (preventer) every morning and evening.

- If I go to play sport, please remind me to take my blue inhaler with me so I can take a dose before I play.

- Encourage me to play sport. As well as keeping me fit, it will help to keep my heart, bones and digestive system healthy, as well as improving my breathing.

Below is a list of Asthma 'triggers', I will need your help to avoid some of these, though only some of them will affect me:

- Animal dander (dead skin and hair, or saliva from cats, which is transferred to their coat when they wash themselves). Note that Asthma is not always triggered by your own pet.

- Bonfire smoke.

- Chemical irritants/cleaning products.

- Cold air/weather and changes in temperature.

- Colds and viral infections.

- Dampness in the house.

- Diet – some food and drinks (especially cold drinks).

- Dust.

- Emotional upset.

- Exercise/sport.

- Fumes.

- Hayfever – can make Asthma worse.

- High humidity.

- House dust mites – 80% of children with Asthma are sensitive to these.

- Laughing.

- Medications – Aspirin (not recommended for children under 12 years), Beta-blockers and NSAIDs.

- Perfume or scented products.
- Pollens:
  - tree pollen – late January–end of June
  - grass pollen – April–September
  - oil seed rape – flowers in May
  - mould spores – May–October
  - most weeds – end of June–beginning of September.
- Thunderstorms.
- Tobacco smoke.
- Traffic pollution.

Here are some things you can do to help me avoid the triggers:

- Please don't use a yellow duster, as it only moves the dust into the air. Use a tightly wrung out cloth which will dampen the dust.

- Regularly vacuum around the edge of my bed mattress. It will help reduce household dust mites (although it will not get rid of them altogether). If you need to replace the vacuum cleaner, it would be helpful if you could buy a high efficiency particulate air filter (HEPA). These types of cleaners return a very low amount of dust to the environment.

- Make sure I'm not using a feather pillow. If needed, special allergen free pillow covers are available.

- Don't put any soft fluffy toys on my bed.

- Wash any soft toys at 60 degrees and that will kill off the dust mites, or put them in a plastic bag in the freezer for 6 hours and then vacuum them to remove the dead dust mites.

- If I have to sleep in a bunk bed at any time, make sure I have the top bunk, so that dust from the top bunk will not drop on me.

- When you need to replace the carpets, it would be great if we could have wooden flooring and keep soft furnishing to a minimum.

- If the pollen count is high, close my bedroom window.

- Don't use aerosol air fresheners.

- Be aware of signs that my Asthma may be getting worse.

- Keep in touch and talk to my teacher regularly.

- Always make sure my inhalers are in date and I have a spare at home and at school.

Most importantly, by understanding about my Asthma you will be able to help, encourage, reassure and support me.
     Thank you!"

Recommended reading, websites and organisations

If you would like to find out more about Asthma, here are some useful books, organisations and websites.

BOOKS FOR CHILDREN

Golding, Theresa (Author), Lucas, Margeaux (Illustrator) (2009) *Abby's Asthma and the Big Race*. Albert Whitman and Co., Illinois, USA and Fitzhenry & Whiteside, Canada.

Maitland Deland, M. (2012) *The Great Katie Kate Offers Answers About Asthma*. Greenleaf Book Group Press, Austin, Texas, USA.

Moore-Mallinos, Jennifer (2007) *I Have Asthma (Let's Talk About It!)*. Barron's Educational Series Inc., Hauppauge, New York, USA.

National Service Centre for Environmental Publications (NSCEP) (2004) *Dusty The Asthma Goldfish and His Asthma Triggers Funbook*. www.epa.gov/nscep.

Weiss, Jonathan H. (Author), Chesworth, Michael D. (Illustrator) (2003) *Breathe Easy, Young People's Guide to Asthma*. Second edition. Magination Press, Washington D.C., USA.

BOOKS FOR PARENTS, CARERS, TEACHERS AND OTHER ADULTS

Asthma UK (2012)
Asthma & My Child, booklet
Asthma in under 5's, booklet
After your child's asthma attack, booklet
My asthma, booklet

Levy, Mark, Weller, Trisha and Hilton, Sean (2006) *Asthma at your fingertips.* Class Publishing, London.

Plottel, Claudia S. and Feldman, Robert B. (2006) *100 Questions & Answers About Your Child's Asthma.* Jones and Bartlett Publishers, Inc., Massachusetts, USA.

Rees, John and Kanabar, Dipak (2006) *ABC of Asthma.* Fifth edition. Blackwell Publishing Ltd., Oxford, UK, Massachusetts, USA and Victoria, Australia.

Simmons, Janice C. and Miller Ratcliffez, Marijo A. (2008) *The "Everything" Parent's Guide to Children with Asthma: Professional Advice to Help Your Child Manage Symptoms, Be More Active, and Breathe Better.* Adams Media, Avon, UK and Massachusetts, USA.

ORGANISATIONS AND WEBSITES
UK
Asthma UK
Summit House
70 Wilson Street
London
EC2A 2DB
Telephone: 0800 121 62 55
Website: www.asthma.org.uk

British Lung Foundation
Website: www.blf.org.uk/Asthma-in-children

The British Thoracic Society
17 Doughty Street
London
WC1N 2PL
Telephone: 020 7831 8778
Website: www.brit-thoracic.org.uk

Department of Health
Richmond House
79 Whitehall
London
SW1A 2NS
Telephone: 020 7210 5952
Website: www.dh.gov.uk/health/contact-dh

USA
Asthma and Allergy Foundation of America
Website: www.aafa.org

CANADA
The Asthma Society of Canada
Website: www.asthma.ca/kids

AUSTRALIA

Asthma Australia
Website: www.asthmaaustralia.org.au

National Asthma Council Australia
Website: www.nationalasthma.org.au

NEW ZEALAND

Asthma Foundation New Zealand
Website: www.asthmanz.co.nz